PRESIDENTIAL DEBATES

PHIL CORSO

PowerKiDS
press.

New York

Published in 2020 by The Rosen Publishing Group, Inc.
29 East 21st Street, New York, NY 10010

First Edition

Editor: Rachel Gintner
Book Design: Tanya Dellaccio

Photo Credits: Cover, pp. 9 (bottom), 25 (bottom) Bloomberg/Getty Images; p. 4 Pool/Getty Images News/Getty Images; p. 5 Ed Clark/The LIFE Picture Collection/Getty Images; p. 7 Chip Somodevilla/Getty Images News/Getty Images; p. 9 (top) Bettman/Getty Images; p. 10 Alex Wong/Getty Images News/Getty Images; p. 11 EMMANUEL DUNAND/AFP/Getty Images; p. 13 (top) UniversalImagesGroup/Getty Images; p. 13 (bottom) Ed Maker/Denver Post/getty Images; p. 15 Time Life Pictures/The LIFE Picture Collection/Getty Images; p. 16 CBS Photo Archive/CBS/Getty Images; p. 17 AFP/Pool/Getty Images; p. 19 PAUL J. RICHARDS/AFP/Getty Images; p. 21 Carolyn Cole/Los Angeles Times/Getty Images; p. 23 Bruce Bennet/Getty Images News/Getty Images; p. 25 (top) Joe Raedle/Getty Images News/Getty Images; p. 27 David McNew/Getty Images News/Getty Images; p. 29 (both) Wally McNamee/Corbis Historical/Getty Images.

Cataloging-in-Publication Data

Names: Corso, Phil.
Title: Presidential debates / Phil Corso.
Description: New York : PowerKids Press, 2020. | Series: U.S. presidential elections: how they work | Includes glossary and index.
Identifiers: ISBN 9781725310902 (pbk.) | ISBN 9781725310926 (library bound) | ISBN 9781725310919 (6 pack)
Subjects: LCSH: Presidents–United States–Election–Juvenile literature. | Elections–United States–Juvenile literature. | Representative government and representation–United States.
Classification: LCC JK1978.C66 2020 | DDC 324.6–dc23

Manufactured in the United States of America

CPSIA Compliance Information: Batch # CWPK20. For Further Information contact Rosen Publishing, New York, New York at 1-800-237-9932.

CONTENTS

A WAR OF IDEAS 4

WHO ENTERS THE RING? 6

DEBATE TRADITIONS 8

DEBATE TIMELINES 10

THE BIG LEAGUES 12

THE GOLDEN ERA OF TV 14

JFK VERSUS NIXON 16

THE BIGGEST BOUTS 18

PRIMARIES COME FIRST 20

DIFFERENT STYLES TO DISH 22

THE RULES OF ENGAGEMENT 24

COMMISSION ON PRESIDENTIAL DEBATES . 26

WHEN POLITICS GET POLITICAL 28

BETTER WAYS TO DEBATE 30

GLOSSARY 31

INDEX 32

WEBSITES 32

A WAR OF IDEAS

In the United States, voters have the ability to choose who leads the country through a process known as elections. But how do they know who to vote for? This is where presidential debates become important.

Throughout the campaign season, candidates typically step onto a debate stage several times to talk about important issues, answer voter questions, and share their visions for the future.

Television opened the door for American voters to meet their presidential candidates through publicized, far-reaching debates.

A NEW PROCESS IN AN OLD COUNTRY

DEBATES ARE STILL A RELATIVELY NEW IDEA IN AMERICAN **DEMOCRACY.** PRESIDENTIAL CANDIDATES USED TO THINK IT WAS A BAD IDEA TO DEBATE THEIR OPPONENTS IN PUBLIC. IT WAS NOT UNTIL THE YEAR 1960, WHEN A TELEVISED DEBATE BETWEEN DEMOCRATIC SENATOR JOHN F. KENNEDY AND REPUBLICAN VICE PRESIDENT RICHARD NIXON PUT THE PROCESS ON TELEVISION. EVEN THEN, IT WAS ANOTHER 16 YEARS UNTIL THE NEXT TELEVISED PRESIDENTIAL DEBATE.

JOHN F. KENNEDY

RICHARD NIXON

Debates start in the "primary" phase, which determines who will lead each party in the general election. After the primary elections, the leaders of each party running for president and vice present debate each other.

But it has not always been done this way. The presidential debate system became a more consistent tradition over recent decades as **technology** has allowed them to be televised.

WHO ENTERS THE RING?

Presidential debates start long before the general election, which takes place every four years in November. Candidates running for president face off in primary debates first, and then the winners of each party's primary election will debate. Each presidential candidate chooses a running mate to serve as their vice president, and these nominees debate as well.

The Commission on Presidential Debates uses a set of rules to assist in picking who's allowed onto the debate stage. In order to be included, candidates must be on the **ballot** in enough states to possibly receive 270 **electoral** votes. That's the number of votes they must win in the general election if they're to win the White House. They also must gain at least 15 percent of the public's support in five major national polls.

The debate format starts in the primary election stage of the electoral process and continues until each party has its winner.

DEBATE TRADITIONS

The American tradition of debates has developed over the centuries since the country's founding. In 1858, for example, Abraham Lincoln challenged Senator Stephen Douglas to seven debates in Illinois. One man gave an hour-long introduction, the other responded for 90 minutes, and the first man closed for another 30 minutes.

Debate traditions have come a long way since then. In modern America, the debate process begins about one year before the general election. Candidates seeking their party's presidential nomination go on television and debate each other for the first time. After each party chooses its candidate, the winners and their running mates debate each other in general election debates.

The events follow different styles, but always focus on some of the country's most important **policy** issues.

Democratic candidate for president Hillary Clinton, right, shakes hands with challenger Bernie Sanders during a 2016 presidential primary debate.

PATH TO THE PRESIDENCY

PRESIDENT JIMMY CARTER REFUSED TO DEBATE REPUBLICAN RONALD REAGAN AND INDEPENDENT JOHN ANDERSON IN 1980. HE FELT THAT BY INCLUDING AN INDEPENDENT CANDIDATE, THERE WOULD BE TOO MANY PEOPLE DEBATING.

JOHN ANDERSON

RONALD REAGAN

DEBATE TIMELINES

While Election Day is not until November, the presidential and vice presidential debate process starts much earlier.

In recent history, the first presidential debates have usually taken place sometime during the month of September, about two months before voters head to the polls. A second debate usually follows in the beginning of October, and another one occurs near the end of the month, just before the November election hits. Vice

Some of the candidates seeking the Republican nomination for president in the 2016 election included Ted Cruz, Marco Rubio, Jeb Bush, and John Kasich, pictured here at a debate in January 2016.

TECHNOLOGY AND DEBATING

THE 2008 PRESIDENTIAL DEBATES BETWEEN DEMOCRAT BARACK OBAMA AND REPUBLICAN JOHN MCCAIN OPENED A NEW DOOR INTO THE FUTURE OF DEBATING BY USING MODERN TECHNOLOGY IN NEW WAYS. IT WAS THE FIRST TIME PRESIDENTIAL CANDIDATES ANSWERED QUESTIONS THAT VOTERS SUBMITTED THEMSELVES ON SOCIAL MEDIA PLATFORMS LIKE YOUTUBE AND FACEBOOK. THAT TREND CONTINUED TO GROW IN THE 2016 PRESIDENTIAL DEBATES, WHEN VOTERS ALSO SUBMITTED QUESTIONS DIRECTLY TO THE CANDIDATES USING TWITTER.

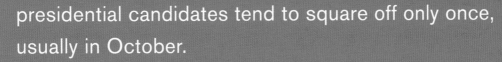

JOHN MCCAIN

BARACK OBAMA

presidential candidates tend to square off only once, usually in October.

The primary debate process starts even earlier. In fact, the first major party primary debates start airing televised debates more than one year before Election Day. This gives voters time to pick which candidate they want to go onto the general election, and that is decided by the summertime.

THE BIG LEAGUES

Organizing presidential debates has not always been easy. The groups who controlled the scheduling and formatting of the events have changed over the decades.

After the Kennedy and Nixon debate, the United States went 16 years without a public debate. But that changed in 1976 when a group called the League of Women Voters stepped in to **sponsor** three debates between Democrat Jimmy Carter and Republican Gerald Ford. They also sponsored a vice presidential debate between Democrat Walter Mondale and Republican Bob Dole that same year.

The League of Women Voters continued to sponsor debates every election year until 1984, when the Democratic and Republican parties decided to start their own group. By 1988, the Commission on Presidential Debates was formed, and they have sponsored every debate since.

Democrat Jimmy Carter and Republican Gerald Ford face off in a 1976 presidential debate sponsored by the League of Women Voters.

JIMMY CARTER

GERALD FORD

PATH TO THE PRESIDENCY

THE COMMISSION ON PRESIDENTIAL DEBATES HAS ORGANIZED EVERY DEBATE SINCE 1988. THE **BIPARTISAN** GROUP'S DUTIES ARE TO PICK WHERE THEY'RE HELD, WHO MODERATES THEM, AND HOW THE DEBATE FORMATS ARE ORGANIZED.

League of Women Vote

THE GOLDEN ERA OF TV

The television made presidential debates a more important part of the election process. Before that, voters only learned about the candidates through newspapers, radio, or in-person campaign events. Once televisions became more popular in homes across the country, televising live debates gave citizens a direct way of hearing from those running for office. New candidate features came into play, such as tone of voice and body language.

The first presidential debate to be televised was in 1960 between Democrat John F. Kennedy and Republican Richard Nixon. But because it was still a new process, the airing of live debates did not return for another 16 years until 1976 between Republican Gerald Ford and Democrat Jimmy Carter. Since then, debates have been televised every election.

The first televised presidential debate aired in 1960 and has become an election year tradition since 1976.

JFK VERSUS NIXON

When thinking about the televising of presidential debates, the very first one in 1960 went down in history as a game-changing event.

The first debate between Democrat John F. Kennedy and Republican Richard Nixon aired on September 26, 1960 and caught the attention of some 70 million Americans.

Republican Richard Nixon and Democrat John F. Kennedy trade jabs at the first televised presidential debate in 1960.

PATH TO THE PRESIDENCY

WHEN THE FIRST DEBATE WAS ON CAMERA, THERE WERE ONLY THREE MAJOR **NETWORKS** THAT DOMINATED THE AIR AND RAN THE EVENT. IN 2016, MORE THAN 14 NETWORKS TELEVISED THE PRESIDENTIAL DEBATE.

It was the first time that physical appearances became a central point of the campaign. At that time, Nixon, who was serving as vice president, was a favorite to win over Kennedy, who was a United States senator. However, Nixon appeared to struggle under pressure in front of the cameras, and he was seen sweating and frowning at the debate. But Kennedy looked young and energetic (he also wore makeup), making him look and sound better prepared.

THE BIGGEST BOUTS

As the first on television, the 1960 debate made history. Other debates that followed would also gain a lot of attention.

The 1980 presidential election between Democrat Jimmy Carter and Republican Ronald Reagan was a record-holder in high viewership before recent elections. According to the Nielsen ratings group, the debate had around 80 million viewers. This was aired across three major networks: ABC, CBS, and NBC. The large audience was considered a

BIG DEBATE BUZZ

THE 2008 VICE PRESIDENTIAL DEBATE BETWEEN JOE BIDEN AND SARAH PALIN WAS ONE OF THE MOST TALKED ABOUT EVENTS OF THE 2008 ELECTION CYCLE. SO MUCH SO, THAT POPULAR COMEDY SHOW "SATURDAY NIGHT LIVE" MADE FUN OF THE DEBATE THE FOLLOWING WEEK, WITH TINA FEY PLAYING PALIN AND JASON SUDEIKIS PLAYING BIDEN. VOTERS WERE INTERESTED IN SEEING THE DEBATE AS BOTH OF THE RUNNING MATES WERE KNOWN TO MISSPEAK UNDER PRESSURE.

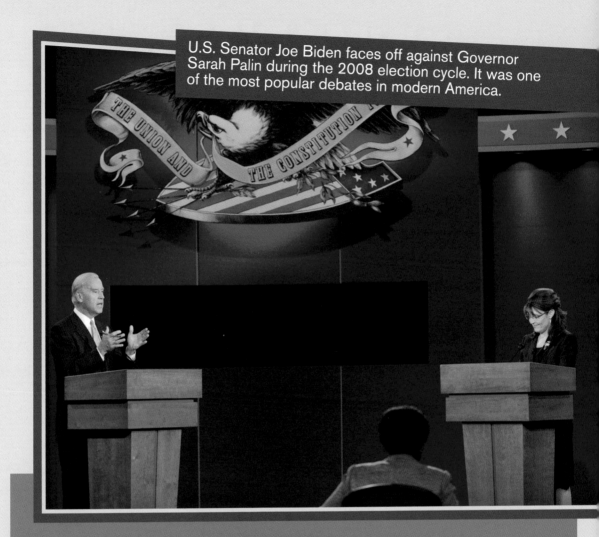

U.S. Senator Joe Biden faces off against Governor Sarah Palin during the 2008 election cycle. It was one of the most popular debates in modern America.

contributing reason to how Reagan was able to beat Carter.

A more modern debate took place in 2008 between presidential running mates Joe Biden, U.S. Senator for Delaware, a Democrat, and Alaska Governor Sarah Palin, a Republican. This was highly anticipated due to confusion and curiosity around political newcomer, Palin.

PRIMARIES COME FIRST

In some ways, presidential primary debates are more important than the final general election debates. Before political parties find out who their candidate for president will be, voters from each party get to vote in elections called primaries. They learn about these candidates through primary debates. Many candidates are running for the same nomination, and choosing the right candidate to face off in the general election is important.

Because the slightest factor could change a voter's mind, primary debates have a high influence on voters. Often, voters already know which party they support, and therefore pay more attention to deciding which candidate to vote for in the primary. Voters have already chosen the party they will vote for later in the general election.

President Donald J. Trump, center, speaks between senators Marco Rubio, left, and Ted Cruz, right, at a Republican primary debate leading up to the 2016 general election.

DIFFERENT STYLES TO DISH

Candidates must agree upon the rules before each debate begins, dealing with factors such as who goes first, where the questions come from, what topics are covered, how much time they have to answer, and whether or not **rebuttals** are given. Every election cycle includes a variety of televised debate traditions.

The debate formats include several popular approaches. The first is the more traditional debate style, in which a moderator asks questions to candidates and gives them a set amount of time for answers and rebuttals. Another style includes sitting the candidates and moderators at the same table to encourage more open discussion. The "town hall" format, which lets voters directly ask the candidates questions, is also popular.

Republican nominee Mitt Romney debates President Barack Obama in a "town hall" debate in October 2012, speaking directly to voters in the room. ▶

THE RULES OF ENGAGEMENT

Candidates are often told about the rules for a debate before it happens so they know what to prepare for. Items that could change from one debate to the next include format, subject matter, and the number of moderators.

For example, when presidential candidates agree to several debates, they might agree to do one focused on a range of important issues or another on only one or two important issues facing the nation.

Participants are told ahead of the debate how much time they will have to speak and what the rules for speaking are. This way, the debate can remain civil without anyone descending to unfair play, such as talking over one another.

PATH TO THE PRESIDENCY

CONGRESS HAD TO SUSPEND A PROVISION OF THE COMMUNICATIONS ACT OF 1934 IN ORDER TO ALLOW JOHN F. KENNEDY AND RICHARD NIXON'S DEBATE TO BE LIMITED TO ONLY THEM.

Before joining the debate stage, candidates agree to a set of rules in order to keep the conversation civil and productive.

COMMISSION ON PRESIDENTIAL DEBATES

Before 1987, the League of Women Voters organized most of the major presidential debates every four years. But both major political parties agreed to establish a nonprofit organization called the Commission on Presidential Debates in the 1980s to take over the process.

Now, the CPD sponsors and produces general election debates every four years and does research to improve them from one year to the next. They also provide technical assistance to other countries around the world, including Nigeria, Peru, Romania, Uganda, and the Ukraine, who are looking to copy the way debates are organized in the United States.

Since its formation, the CPD has hosted debates in 1988, 1992, 1996, 2000, 2004, 2008, 2012, and 2016 with plans to sponsor others for the 2020 presidential campaign.

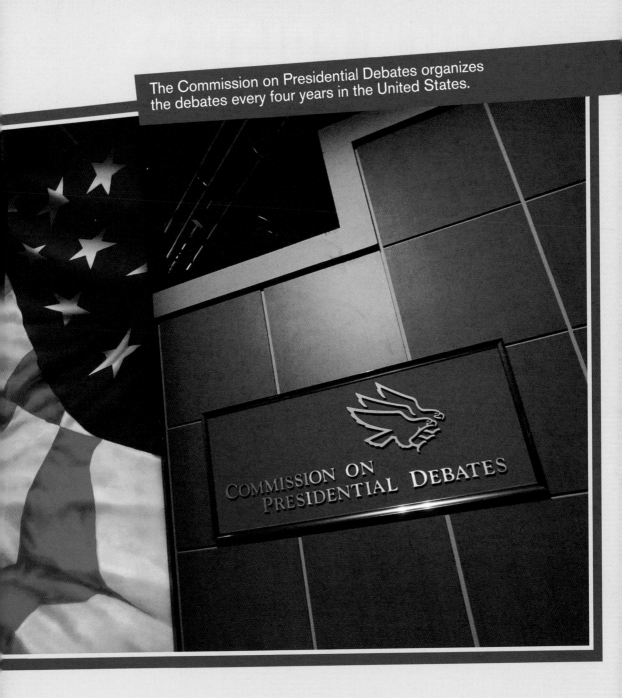

The Commission on Presidential Debates organizes the debates every four years in the United States.

WHEN POLITICS GET POLITICAL

Not everyone has been on board with the way the United States hosts debates. Voters will voice their opinions every election on whether or not the debates did a fair job of presenting the candidates.

One common criticism is that presidential campaign seasons go on for too long, with primary debates starting more than one year before the general election. This, some argue, turns the campaign season into a personality contest, more than a debate about policy.

Some feel that debates focus too heavily on performance, rather than on substance. Viewers will crown a "winning" candidate based on how they delivered their answers, rather than on what they actually said. Others say the debates do little to show how a leader would respond in a crisis, or emergency.

Some people say that hosting debates on television does little to show how the candidates might lead as president.

PATH TO THE PRESIDENCY

ALONG WITH DEMOCRATIC GOVERNOR BILL CLINTON AND REPUBLICAN PRESIDENT GEORGE H. W. BUSH, THE 1992 PRESIDENTIAL DEBATES ALSO FEATURED THIRD-PARTY CANDIDATE ROSS PEROT, AN INDEPENDENT. CLINTON WON THAT ELECTION.

BETTER WAYS TO DEBATE

Many people complain about the country's presidential debate system. Some have offered ideas on how to make them better. Improvements include shortening campaign seasons, having fewer and shorter debates, or simply eliminating them altogether.

One proposal is replacing debates with a more **realistic** event for candidates. In an opinion article in the *Washington Post,* author Lee Drutman suggested giving the candidates crisis **simulations** instead of debates. He wrote, "Great presidents make the right calls in moments of crisis. They reason through unexpected problems. They ask good questions and sort new information quickly. They…thoughtfully weigh trade-offs. A crisis simulation would test these qualities in ways the debate format obviously does not."

Debates are one way Americans currently learn about candidates, but that may not be the way of the future. Perhaps other avenues will emerge.

GLOSSARY

ballot: A paper or electronic form for secure voting.

bipartisan: Of, or relating to, two political parties.

democracy: A government elected by the people, directly or indirectly.

electoral: Relating to elections of electors.

network: A radio or television company that offers programs to broadcast, or deliver.

policy: A course of action a government, party, business, or individual may take.

realistic: Showing a sensible or practical idea of what can be achieved.

rebuttal: An argument against something.

simulation: A representation of the operation of a process by means of another system.

sponsor: When a person or organization hosts, funds, or supports items such as events.

technology: Technical or advanced systems housing information or communication.

INDEX

B
BIDEN, JOE, 18, 19

C
CARTER, JIMMY, 18
COMMISSION ON
PRESIDENTIAL DEBATES, 6,
 12, 13, 26
CRISIS SIMULATIONS, 30

K
KENNEDY, JOHN F., 16, 17

L
LEAGUE OF WOMEN
 VOTERS, 12, 26

N
NIELSEN RATINGS, 18
NIXON, RICHARD, 16, 17

P
PALIN, SARAH, 18, 19
PRIMARIES, 20

R
REAGAN, RONALD, 18
REBUTTAL, 22
RULES, 24

T
TOWN HALL FORMAT, 22

WEBSITES

Due to the changing nature of Internet links, PowerKids Press has developed an online list of websites related to the subject of this book. This site is updated regularly. Please use this link to access the list: www.powerkidslinks.com/uspe/debates